1   Kersal Moor: the heather slopes, *c.* 1900

2   *Following page* Civic and Commercial Buildings, Manchester Assize Courts and a line of hansom cabs.
Architect: Alfred Waterhouse. Begun in 1859. Its main hall was described by Ruskin as 'the most truly
magnificent Gothic apartment in Europe'. The building was destroyed during the Second World War.
At the Social Science Congress in the Assizes in 1866, Lord Brougham was delivering an address when
his dental fixtures fell out, according to the reminiscences 1840–1905 of L. M. Hayes

Victorian and Edwardian

MANCHESTER

and East Lancashire

from old photographs

Introduction and commentaries by
GEORGE CHANDLER

B. T. BATSFORD LTD.
LONDON

First published 1974
Text © George Chandler 1974

ISBN 0 7134 2792 2

04738008

45001393

Filmset by Servis Filmsetting Ltd, Manchester
Printed in Great Britain by
Alden & Mowbray Ltd, Oxford
for the publishers B. T. Batsford Ltd
4 Fitzhardinge Street, London W1H 0AH

CONTENTS

3   The river Irwell from Blackfriars Bridge, 1859

ACKNOWLEDGMENTS

In response to the publisher's invitation, my original intention was to devote a volume in this series to Lancashire, but the richness of the photographic collections, mainly in public libraries, compelled me to divide the work into two volumes. The companion to this volume, looked at the North West mainly from the point of view of the great port of Liverpool and from Western Lancashire up to Preston. This volume is concerned mainly with the great industrial centre of Manchester and with South and North East Lancashire up to Blackburn.

Thanks are due to the public librarians and their staffs who kindly made a preliminary selection from their collections, and to my wife for making a further selection and for her visits to a number of libraries to fill gaps, and for her secretarial and research assistance.

I regret that I could only use a small selection of the available photographs and that there were few available to cover certain social topics, particularly in the early Victorian era. Thanks are due to the city librarian of Manchester and his staff for permission to use the following photographs, which comprise over one quarter of the total: Figs. 7, 9, 17, 20, 22, 24–9, 63–4, 67–8, 69–72, 77, 84, 86–8, 107–10, 114–16, 118–20, 122, 125, 130–1, 134, 142, 149, 151, 153. The Radio Times Hulton Picture Library has kindly provided Figs. 10, 78–9, 92, 100–2, 126–8, 132–3. Other public libraries have provided important photographs: Accrington (Fig. 65); Ashton-under-Lyne (Figs. 48, 85, 97, 124, 143); Atherton (Figs. 59, 99); Bacup (Fig. 90); Blackburn (Figs. 30, 129, 148); Bolton (Figs. 31–3, 112, 137); Burnley (Figs. 35, 106, 123); Bury (Figs. 36, 38, 135); Chorley (Figs. 49, 83); Darwen (Fig. 66); Heywood (Fig. 50); Lancashire (Figs. 23, 34, 144, 145); Liverpool (Figs. 4, 8, 12, 16, 42, 80–1); Middleton (Figs. 51–3, 89, 94–5, 141); Rawtenstall (Figs. 54–6, 82, 96, 138, 140, 146–7, 150); Salford (Figs. 37, 43–6, 93, 103–4, 113, 152); Stretford (Figs. 57, 61, 73–6, 139); Swinton and Pendlebury (Figs. 58, 60, 105, 111, 117, 121); and Wigan (Figs. 47, 91, 98). The remaining photographs came from the publisher's collection.

G. Chandler.

INTRODUCTION

4   Market place and the Old Exchange, 1859

'Manchester is as great a human exploit as Athens', wrote Disraeli in *Coningsby* at the commencement of the Victorian era, but the great civic and commercial buildings of Manchester were erected much later – the Assize Courts (1859) (Fig. 2) and the Town Hall (1868) (Fig. 6). The Manchester Ship Canal (Figs. 73–81) was not opened until 1894. The rebuilding of the central streets (Figs. 7–13) also took place later in the Victorian era. Disraeli was not, therefore, describing Manchester's civic and commercial buildings but its industrial erections which impressed many foreign visitors. A Swiss traveller wrote from Manchester in 1814: 'It is impossible to describe the magnificent appearance of a mill with 256 windows all alight as though the most brilliant sunshine was streaming through them.' In 1842 a chimney $367\frac{1}{2}$ feet high was built at Blinkhorn's chemical works at Bolton and described as 'unparalleled in the world'. Phillips and Lee of Salford had lit their factory with gas since 1805, when the cost of £2,000 per annum for candles was reduced to £600 for gas. Electric light was first introduced on 8 August 1850:

> *Dear Jones at Pendleton last night,*
> *I saw the famed Electric Light,*
> *And as I know you rather doubt it*
> *I write to tell you all about it.*

Although the first photographic studio in Manchester was opened in 1841, the early pioneers did not take photographs of the 'unforgettable sight of great mills shining in the darkness with the light of innumerable lamps' but some surviving panoramic views of Lancashire cotton towns (Fig. 39) do at least reveal that the mills dominated the Lancashire towns as much as Athens was dominated by its marble columns. Perhaps this was the reason why Disraeli claimed that Manchester was comparable with Athens for its human exploits.

There was, of course, another side to Manchester. This too was symbolised by Disraeli. In *Sybil* (1845) he refers to the rich and the poor as 'two nations between whom there is no intercourse and no sympathy'. Friedrich Engels, who came to Manchester in 1842 to join his father's firm of Ermen and Engels, described the terrible conditions of Manchester's poor in *The Conditions of Working-classes in England in 1844*. No early photographs of the poor have been traced, and the later photographs (Figs. 109–19) reveal that the situation, though still unacceptable, had substantially improved. This improvement was not due to a successful revolution, which Engels tried to promote through his joint authorship with Karl Marx of the Communist Manifesto of 1848: 'Workers of the world unite, you have nothing to lose but your chains.' Engels exercised some influence on the Chartists but failed to impel them in the direction of Revolution. The massive improvements in the conditions of the working classes during the Victorian era were due to the influence of religion and social reformers (Figs. 120–31).

Reformers

The first important reform of the Victorian era in Manchester was the incorporation of the borough in 1838 for which Richard Cobden (Fig. 126) had campaigned and of whose council he was a member. Other members included John Edward Taylor, founder of the *Manchester Guardian* and Sir Benjamin Heywood, banker, M.P. for Lancashire and philanthropist.

Cobden had founded a calico printing business in Manchester and was also successful in 1846 in his campaign for the repeal of the Corn Laws in order to reduce the price of food for the distressed workers. Disraeli coined the phrase the Manchester School to describe the group of successful reformers in the Anti-Corn Law League. To mark the repeal, the Free Trade Hall was built in Manchester. It was here that Charles Hallé (Fig. 132) gave a series of concerts in 1858 which led eventually to the foundation of the Hallé Orchestra. Hallé had been born in Westphalia and was invited to come to Manchester by Hermann Leo, a Lancashire cotton printer. Hallé's influence in the reform of the cultural life of Manchester was great.

Another great reformer Sir Joseph Whitworth (Fig. 127) was appointed manager of his uncle's cotton mill at the age of 18 and founded his own engineering works. In 1868 he established his famous engineering scholarships – a pioneer recognition before the Education Act of 1870 that the development of industry required higher educational training.

Later in the Victorian era reform took another direction through Emmeline Pankhurst, daughter of a Manchester calico printer, who helped to found the Women's Franchise League in 1889. This was, as the photograph (Fig. 130), suggests, a middle class movement.

Religion

Religion was the driving force behind many of these reforms. John Bright was a Quaker. Sir Benjamin Heywood was the son of a leading Unitarian from Liverpool.

Edward Baines reported in 1843 in his *The Social, Educational and Religious State of the Manufacturing Districts* that there was a church or chapel room for over 42% of the population in Lancashire as compared with 30% in London. There was a Sunday school attender for $5\frac{2}{3}$ inhabitants in Lancashire as compared with one out of twenty in London.

The photographs (Fig. 123) show that the churches and chapels organised excursions and music recitals and were centres of social life. The annual Whit Week procession was so widely observed in Lancashire that business was dislocated for a whole week.

When Roger Oldham published his *Manchester Alphabet* (1906) the Whit Week Walk was chosen to represent the letter W:

> *The scholars' walk in Manchester*
> *Is quite a pretty sight,*
> *The boys have all their faces washed,*
> *Their boots with blacking bright,*
> *The girls all have their hair in curl,*
> *Their dresses spotless white.*

The relief agencies established by the churches and chapels did much to alleviate the conditions of the underprivileged (Figs. 118–19).

Through the Sunday schools religious bodies played an important part in the development of education, preparing the ground for the first compulsory Education Act of 1870.

The churches were also active in the Temperance movement, using all available media to press their message:

> *I'm very fond of a social glass*
> *But it must be filled with water;*
> *Water pure doth brighter shine*
> *Than brandy, rum or sparkling wine.*

Industry and Occupations

The success of the reformers is perhaps most clearly indicated in the surviving photographs of the workers in the late Victorian and Edwardian eras. There are few signs of the terrible conditions of 50 years earlier before the Factory Acts became effective.

The mill girls (Fig. 89) and the pit brow lassies (Fig. 98) are healthy looking, well clad and buxom. The bricklayers (Figs. 103–4) are wearing bowler hats. The industrial workers are decently clad. Even the strike scenes reveal only occasionally the remnants of a former dire poverty: the photograph of the show of hands during the Salford dock strike of 1907 includes only one boy in bare feet (Fig. 113). Indeed the photographs of the industrial workers and the transport operatives (Fig. 65) reveal pride and satisfaction, and not only in connection with important developments pioneered in Manchester such as Nasmyth's Steam Hammer, Rolls Royce and the Manchester Ship Canal (Figs. 107–8).

Even the doggerel written in connection with strikers is free from bitterness and is couched in religious terms of repentance:

> *We ask now trade is good again, that employers should repent*
> *And give us back without delay the advance of Ten per Cent.*

This was sung during the Haslingden Cotton Mill Strike of 1853.

Culture and Leisure

The Sunday schools had fostered the addiction to reading which observers remarked was a feature of many of the working classes. Samuel Bamford (Fig. 125) recorded in his *Walks in South Lancashire* (1844) that 'the working class of South Lancashire are the greatest readers; can show the greatest numbers of writers; the greatest number of sensible and considerate public speakers'. Mrs Gaskell recorded in *Mary Barton* (1848) that in the neighbourhood of Oldham there were weavers with Newton's *Principia* 'open on their looms'.

The need to have improved access to literature led to the foundation of libraries by mechanics' institutes and similar bodies. Eventually the increasing demand for literature resulted in the establishment of pioneer British public library committees or services in three Lancashire towns – Liverpool, Manchester and Warrington, each of which has claim from some point of view to have

been the national pioneer of public libraries. The photograph (Fig. 137) of a children's library in the 1890's reveals the popularity of books and the seriousness of their readers. The pursuit of learning is symbolised in the murals in the Manchester Town Hall, which includes one of John Daltons:

John Dalton lived in Manchester
A hundred years ago,
A famous scientific man
As all the world doth know.

Some of the early public libraries were also associated with art galleries, but it was the Exhibition of Art Treasures in Manchester in 1857 which gave a great fillip to the fine arts. The picture of Queen Victoria at the Exhibition is a notable early photograph (Fig. 134).

Later in the century the foundation of art galleries became an important object of social reformers. Opening ceremonies were great occasions (Fig. 135).

There were a number of developments in the field of music. As early as 1835 George Hogarth wrote in his *Musical History* that 'in the densely populated manufacturing districts music is cultivated among the working classes to an extent unparalleled in any other part of the country'. In 1862, during the terrible stress of the Cotton Famine of the American Civil War, Edwin Waugh (1817–1890) wrote that 'the great works of Handel, Haydn, Beethoven and Mozart have solaced the toil of thousands of the poorest workpeople of Lancashire . . . it is not uncommon to meet working men wandering over the hills with their musical instruments to take part in some village oratorio many miles away'.

The photographs of musical bands and concert parties are revealing (Figs. 138–40). The pursuit of cultural activities was possible even when long hours were worked, because they did not make heavy demands on physical energies. The development of sport had to await the reduction in hours of work.

Sports and Recreations

After the Ten Hours Act of 1857 the number of working hours was, in many cases, reduced considerably and this freed energies to devote to sports. A Blackburn mill worker referred in 1849 to the consequences of the Ten Hours Act: 'It is only now that operatives can enjoy gardens . . . formerly they could not take a walk in the mill yard, but were locked inside the mill from five in the morning till nine at night.' The opening of public parks attracted large crowds (Fig. 150).

Hours of work continued to be long by modern standards, and for most workers strolls in parks were sufficient. The younger and more active turned to the sports which were developed in the Victorian era. Church and chapel had combined to condemn sports and recreations at the beginning of the Victorian period: all the restricted leisure time was required for religious services and social reform. In 1832 the Primitive Methodists of Haslingden decided to expel Sunday school teachers who persisted in 'frequenting public houses, card tables, dancing rooms, cricket playing or gaming of any kind'. Nevertheless, the first cricket match at Bolton in 1839 attracted a 'numerous party of ladies and gentlemen', while the match between Preston and Burnley in Burnley's new ground in July 1833 drew 'a large concourse of spectators' and 'gave the fair sex an opportunity of observing this manly game'.

The rules of the Haslingden Cricket Club founded in 1853 forbade wagering, 'however trivial'. A fielder lying down or smoking during the match was fined 6d. The Preston New Cricket Club, founded in 1837, laid down that the uniform 'shall be a blue cap, white flannel jacket trimmed with blue, belt of navy blue leather $2\frac{1}{4}''$ wide and white trousers'. The surviving photographs confirm that the dress for cricket was still not standard (Figs. 143–5).

Cycling was developed as a most popular recreation. At the opening of the Haslingden Athletic Club in 1869, some 8,000 people, including 'a number of fashionably dressed ladies and gentlemen', watched a number of sports including bicycle and velocipede racing. The machines were 'of various builds'. Their 'jockeys' managed 'their iron steeds with great skill and pace'. Many of the machines of working men were made by their owners. The photographs of the cyclists (Figs. 146–7) show their satisfaction and sense of achievement. Certainly the development of sports in the later Victorian and Edwardian eras provided many outlets for the energy and enthusiasm of the working classes and reinforced the work of the social reformers in bridging the gaps between the two nations of industrial Lancashire.

CITY OF MANCHESTER

In Manchester, this famous town,
What great improvements have been made, sirs,
In fifty years 'tis mighty grown,
All owing to success in trade, sirs: . . .
'Tis coal and cotton boil the pot, sirs –
Richard Baines

6   Manchester Town Hall, Albert Square, 1880. Architect: Alfred Waterhouse. Work commenced in 1868. Opened officially on 13 September 1877. The Ford Madox Brown murals were added later. One of these was devoted to Dalton:

Historical scenes of Manchester town
Were painted in fresco by Ford Madox Brown.
A fresco is something that can't run away,
It's stuck on the plaster for ever and aye –
Roger Oldham, *Manchester Alphabet* (1906)

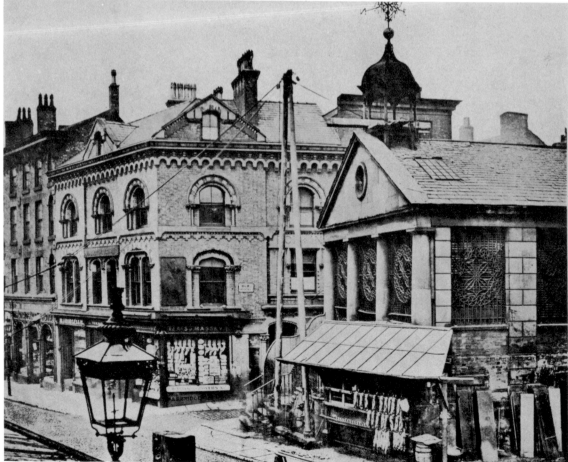

7 *Left* Piccadilly, *c.* 1885 'New buildings have replaced the old . . . the old Infirmary pond has long ago vanished to be replaced afterwards with a wide esplanade . . . where many of our city statues have been provided with a home' – L. M. Hayes in 1905

8 *Below left* Victoria Fish Market, Victoria Street, 1860. 'On the other side of Deansgate on a portion of the ground now covered by the Victoria Hotel, there stood the old Victoria Market . . . a very primitive sort of place just open wooden stalls, with narrow passages between' – L. M. Hayes in 1905

9 *Below* Deansgate 1884. 'When Deansgate was widened and improved large blocks of old shops and buildings were cleared away. . . . There used to be numerous hovels for carts and lorries. At night times the courts were dimly lit . . . a small flickering lamp or gas jet to make darkness visible' – L. M. Hayes in 1905

10 *Left* Market Street, 1864. 'The street to-day is still far too narrow and confined... on the whole the general features of Market Street have not varied very materially' – L. M. Hayes in 1905

11 *Above* Portland Street. 'The change is wonderful.... I can quite well remember when the far greater proportion of Portland Street consisted of low-roofed houses and shops, dirty, decayed-looking and dingy' – L. M. Hayes in 1905

12   The Old Town Hall, 1875. The Reference Library was at one time housed in the Old Town Hall

3   King Street. 'King Street was going to be paved with setts. The Banks were in favour of Macadam being continued' – J. H. S. Crompton, manager of the Lancashire and Yorkshire Bank, in his unpublished diary for 11 March 1889

14 Old House, Smithy Door,
Manchester, 1875

15 *Left* Grosvenor Hotel

16 *Below left* St Ann's Church, Manchester, consecrated 1712. This photograph was taken in 1863

17 *Above* Lower Mosley Street looking towards St Peter's Church, 5 March 1897. The city war memorial now stands on the site of St Peter's

MANCHESTER MARKETS AND STREETS

18   Smithfield Market, 1897

19   Market Place seen from the Royal Exchange, 1883

20 *Left* The Shambles, *c.* 1895

21 *Below left* Long Millgate. Note the shop signs: Tea, Bovril, Coffee; Victoria Coffee House; Mrs E. King confectioner; Derby Commercial House; Tea and Coffee Rooms; Printing Works

22 *Below* Marks and Spencer Original Penny Bazaar, Stretford Street. Admission free. Note that inflation was already in operation. On left 'Any Article this Section 1½d'; on right 'Any Article this Section 1d'

23 Market Street, *c.* 1911. Note shops: China Tea; Electrical Supplies; Chamber and Co. Practical Angler; Coal Exchange; Central Registry Office for Servants

25 Congested traffic in Corporation Street, Market Street Corner, *c.* 190

24 Royal procession, Stretford Road 1905. Edward VII and Queen Alexandra

26 Pedestrians in Market Street
– Corner of High Street, 1894.
Note the boy selling *Spy*

27 *Below* Market Street, 1894. Two men in bowlers, a woman in a cape

28 *Right* Pedestrians in Oldham Street. Note only one top hat, three bowlers, only one woman in shawl, three well dressed

29 *Below right* Pedestrians in Piccadilly

COUNTY BOROUGHS

30   *Above* Blackburn, Pickering the brushmaker 37 Church Street, 1870

31   *Above right* Bolton Arch and line of hansom cabs

32   *Below right* Bolton. Crowds in Square

33 *Right* Bolton. Church

34 *Below* Burnley-Manchester Road

35 *Far right* Burnley. Civic procession in Church Street for the Coronation of King Edward VII

36 *Below right* Bury. The Rock, Fleet Street. P. Hardman Fishmonger, Oyster Dealer

39 *Below* Rochdale. View showing mills

40 *Below* Rochdale. View from Town Hall Square

42 *Left* Rochdale. The Church steps, 1912

43 *Below* Salford. Victoria Park, 1866

44 *Bottom* Salford. Archway over Regent Road built to commemorate the opening of the Manchester Ship Canal, 1894

45 *Below* Salford. Docks, 1895

46 *Right* Salford. Old houses, Greengate. Opposite Bull's Head, 1898

47 *Below right* Wigan. Standishgate between Church Street and New Square about 1875. Note the butcher's shop with meat on the open counter

BOROUGHS AND URBAN DISTRICTS

'One huge congerie of villages, thickening ever and anon into towns . . . the line of railway is almost everywhere fringed with factories and houses.' Bryce, 1868

48 Ashton-under-Lyne. Cavalry on the way to their barracks. Moving along Katherine Street (Penny Meadows) *c.* 1900. Photograph taken from the side of the Town Hall. The Market Hall is on the right

49 Chorley. Anderton Street, decorated for Queen Victoria's Diamond Jubilee, 1899, with banners 'Good Old England' and 'Bless our Queen'

Market St Heywood

50 *Left* Heywood. Market Street, c. 1910

51 *Below left* Middleton. The Old Toll Bar facing the White Hart, Birch, demolished when Langley Lane was widened. Photographed *c.* 1865. Policeman Wise is standing in the centre. In the middle of the gateway is Tom Elliott the clogger. The boy leaning is Tom Jacques who later became the schoolmaster of Birch

52 *Below* Middleton. The Olde Boar's Head, *c.* 1870

53 *Right* Middleton. Tonge Hall, 1894

54 *Below* Rawtenstall. Queen's Square, *c.* 1910, and a portion of Bacup Road. Queen's Hotel front left

55 Rawtenstall. The Fold, *c.* 1910

56 Rossendale. Bank Street, 1897, decorated with banner 'Our Colonies'

58 Swinton and Pendlebury. Off to the Derby. How some residents of Pendlebury celebrated Queen Victoria's Diamond Jubilee in 1900

Left Stretford. The Old Cock Inn and the horse omnibus terminus

TRANSPORT

59 Gib Fold Farm, Atherton, *c.* 1910. Pony and trap. J. Baxendale the driver. The farm was demolished in June 1956

60 Manchester Carriage Company Limited. Founded c. 1865. Its three horse buses travelled down most of the main roads. This bus operated between Ashton, Fairfield, Openshaw, Market Street, Peel Park and Pendleton. Note that eight of these early passengers of horse buses are wearing top hats and only one a bowler. 'The omnibuses had a musty smell with wisps of straw placed under the feet in wet weather, which gave the interior a strong flavour of the stalls', according to the reminiscences (1840–1905) of L. M. Hayes

61 Manchester Carriage and Tramways Company. Horse tram in Chorlton Road, Stretford, connecting All Saints, Stretford Road and Brooks's Bar. The tram drivers 'had to unyoke their horses on arrival at the terminus and to walk round to the other end of the tram until Mr Eade introduced his patent revolving car for the Manchester Carriage Company' – L. M. Hayes in 1905

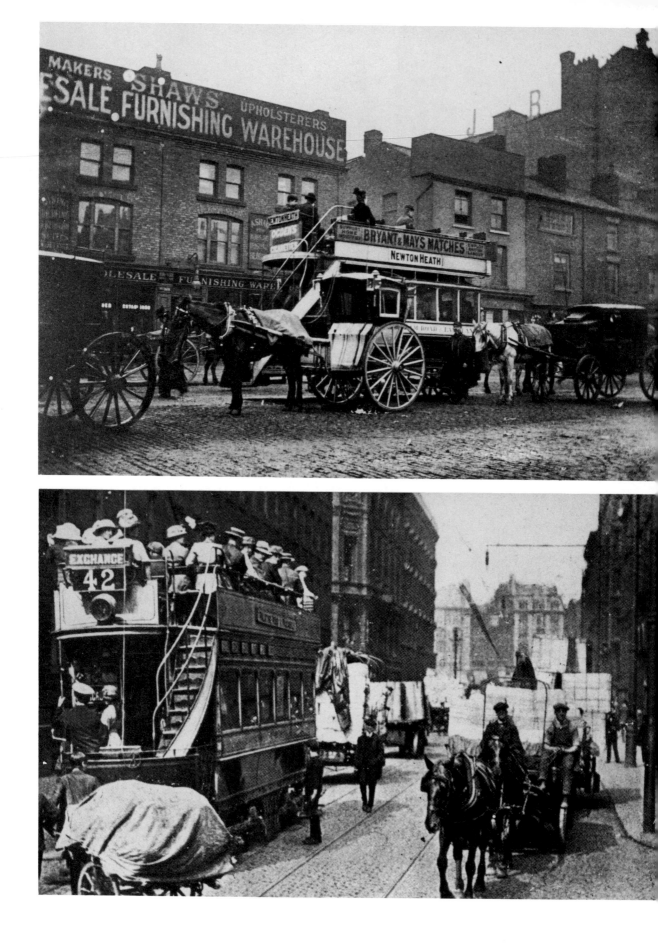

62 *Left* Hansom cabs and tram car with advertisements for Ogden's cigarettes and Bryant and May's matches. The first cabstand was established in Piccadilly in 1839 by William White and cabs were called growlers because of the noise they made on the cobble stones, according to the reminiscences 1840–1905 of L. M. Hayes

63 *Below left* Tram car 42 in Portland Street, Manchester, looking North from Sackville Street. Bound for Exchange

64 *Below* Manchester Corporation Tramways Parcels Van No. 1, 17 February 1905

65 *Following page* End of Accrington's Baltic Fleet, July 1907

End Of Accrington'

Baltic Fleet July 1907.

66 *Left* Sough. Railway station, Spring Vale, a paper mill halt on the L.M.S. Railway 1½ miles South of Darwen, *c.* 1868. 'Trains stopped at every little place on the way; you were shunted here and shunted there' – L. M. Hayes in 1905

67 *Below left* Manchester, Victoria Railway Station of the Lancashire and Yorkshire Railway Company, *c.* 1870. Note the hansom cabs. 'What would the young people of the present time think of having to do without their hansom to sport about in when they are often times too lazy to walk' – L. M. Hayes in 1905

68 *Below* Central Station, Manchester

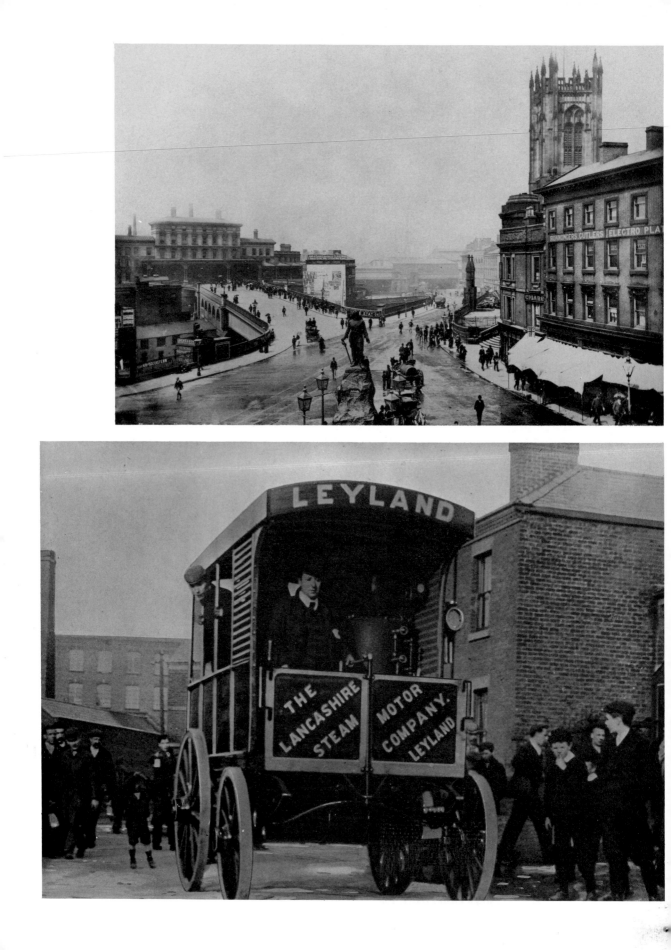

69 *Left* Railway Station, Manchester, from the Victoria Hotel, 1880

70 *Below left* The Lancashire Steam Motor Company Leyland. First steam van, 1896

71 *Below* Two-cylinder Rolls Royce car 10 h.p., *c.* 1905

MANCHESTER SHIP CANAL

The Canal took six years to build. It is $35\frac{1}{2}$ miles long, 28 feet deep and has a width of 120 feet at the bottom

73   One-arm man pitching

74   *Right* Facing work at Mode Wheel

75 *Left* Workmen using a hydraulic riveting machine

76 *Right* Rock getting, Lower Walton

77 *Below* Use of horses in construction work, *c.* 1890

78 *Following page* Letting in the water at Ellesmere Port. E. L. Williams and other engineers

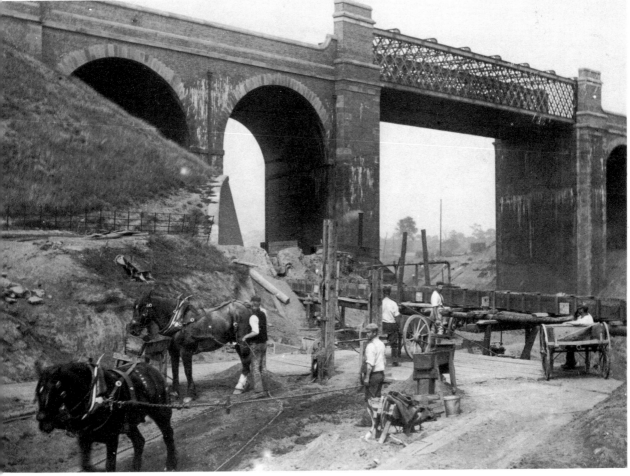

79 *Right* Opening of Manchester Ship Canal, 1 January 1894. The Norseman leading from Latchford

80 *Below* Shipping in Manchester Ship Canal, *c.* 1895

81 *Left* The Docks, Manchester
Ship Canal, 1896

PUBLIC SERVICES

82   Building the Clough Bottan Reservoir, *c.* 1895, Rawtenstall

83 The Gas Works Float showing street lighting. Chorley, *c.* 1870

84 Telegraph Office. The Telephone Room, King Street, Manchester

85 *Right* Postmen of Ashton-under-Lyne, 1905. The ribbon bands on the uniforms denote the period of service in the Post Office

86 *Below* Manchester Grand Theatre of Varieties, Peter Street, *c.* 1900. Fire fighting

88 Policeman off duty in the 1850's

OCCUPATIONS

89   Mill girls, Irk Mill, Middleton, 1903

90 *Below* 'Putting a Cop On' Lancashire cotton weaving. Bacup.

91 *Right* Wigan mill girls card room, *c.* 1900

92 *Below right* Girls in a hatting factory, 1900–1910

"Puttin' a Cop On." Lancs Cotton Wearing.

WIGAN MILL GIRLS, CARD-ROOM.

93   Weavers, 1895

94 *Left* Bobbin winding – silk, *c.* 1903

96 *Right* A mill fire brigade, *c.* 1900

97 *Below right* Horse omnibus of the defunct Manchester Horse Tramway Company crossing Katherine Street, Ashton-under-Lyne, 1904, taking imported workers to the strike-bound Curzon Mill. Escort provided by the Ashton Borough Police

95 *Right* Handloom weaving – silk, *c.* 1903

'In Lancashire, particularly in Manchester, is to be found not only the origin but the heart of the industry of the United Kingdom' – *The Condition of the Working Classes*, by Friedrich Engels

PIT BROW GIRLS 1.

98   Pit brow girls, *c.* 1903, Wigan

99 The Gibfield lamp room, *c.* 1906, Atherton

100 Wigan colliery disaster.
Scene at No. 2 shaft, 19 August
1908

101 *Above* Wives and relatives waiting for news, 19 August 1908

102 *Left* Wigan colliery disaster. Fairhurst with wife and child, 19 August 1908

103   Bricklayers with bowler hats at work, Salford, 1895

104 Bricklayers in caps at work, Salford, 1895

105 Gerrard's joinery shop, Swinton and Pendlebury, *c.* 1900

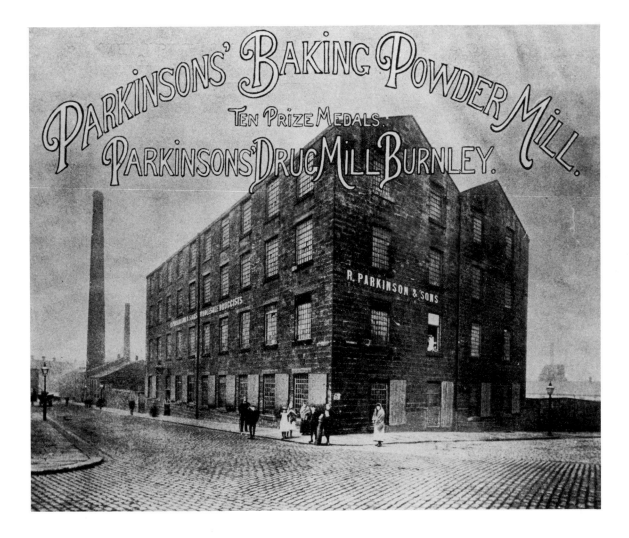

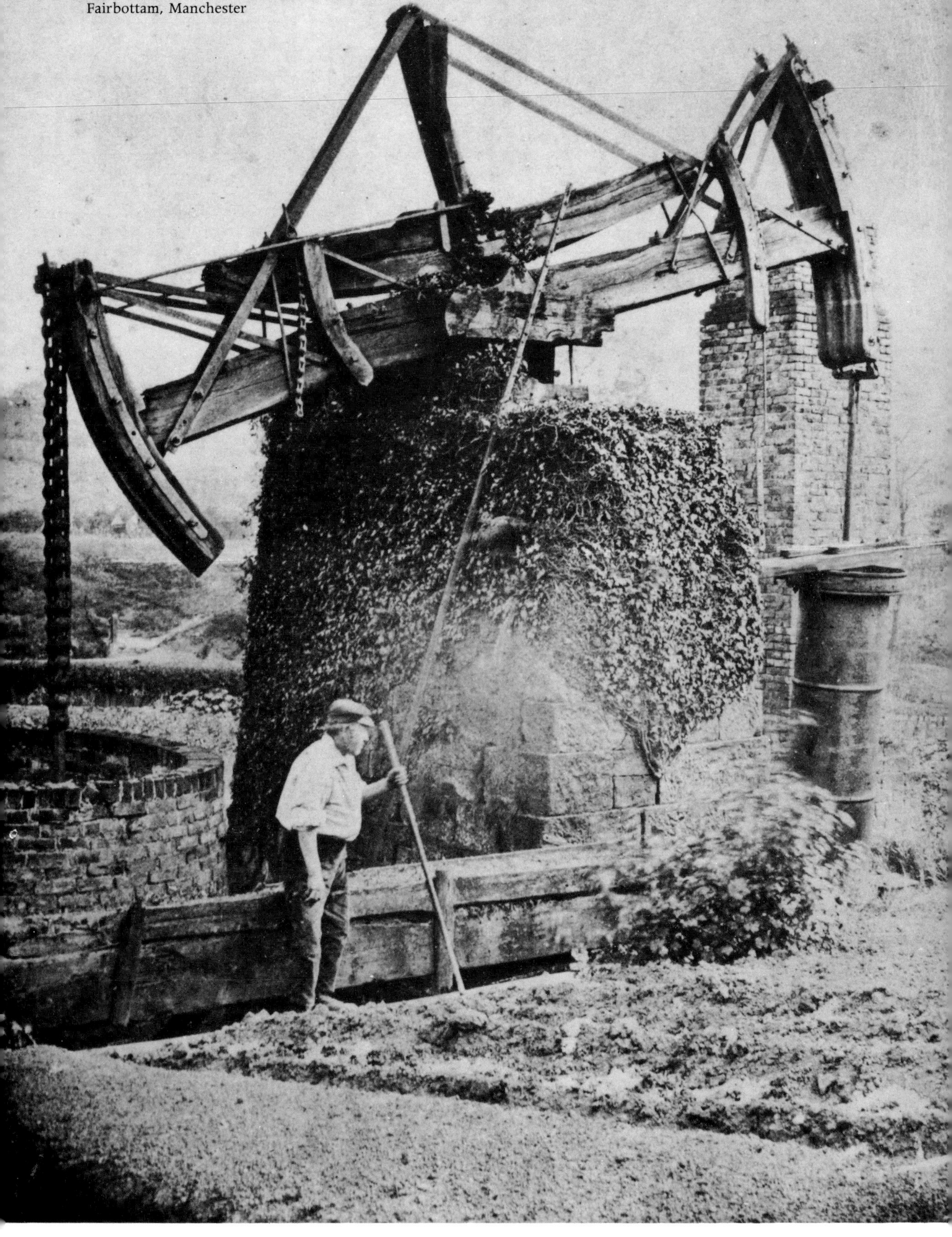

107 Watt's first engine, Fairbottam, Manchester

108 Nasmyth's steam hammer, 1855. James Nasmyth on the platform, Manchester

THE UNDERPRIVILEGED

'Sickness and mortality has been reduced to an extent that is almost incredible. . . . The young men and maidens employed in the mills are now as robust as the families of the indolent classes' – W. A. Abram, editor of the *Blackburn Times*, writing in 1868

109   The Central Hall, Manchester, Workmen's Shop: Pott Street Labour Yard, *c.* 1895. From the reports of the Manchester and Salford Wesleyan Mission 1893–1907

110 Interior of the Labour Yard, Ancoats. Firewood chopping. From the reports of the Manchester and Salford Wesleyan Mission 1893–1907

111 Swinton Industrial Schools, *c.* 1903

114 Organ grinder, *c.* 1895, and poor children

113 *Left* Salford Dock Strike. A show of hands, 1907

115 *Left* Newspaper seller – Relief of Ladysmith, 1900

116 *Right* Destitute children at the Central Hall, Manchester. From the reports of the Manchester and Salford Wesleyan Mission 1893–1907

117 *Below* Salford Union Workhouse. Girls with shaven heads

118 Coffee tavern in Woman's
Home. From the reports of the
Manchester and Salford
Wesleyan Mission, 1893–1907

119 Sister Pattie in the Advice
Bureau, Central Hall, Manchester.
From the reports of the Manchester
and Salford Wesleyan Mission,
1893–1907

RELIGION

'Long before even enlightened statesmen and leaders of public opinion cared for the education of the peoples, the congregations had begun to work in the Sunday schools' – Sir James Kay-Shuttleworth in 1867

120 Open air Methodist service in Stevenson Square, Manchester. From the reports of the Manchester and Salford Wesleyan Mission, 1893–1907

121 *Above* Moorside Independent Methodist Church, Swinton and Pendlebury. Sunday school procession, *c.* 1905

122 *Left* Manchester. Lever Street Sunday School's first missioners. From the reports of the Manchester and Salford Wesleyan Mission, 1893–1907

123 *Above right* Burnley. St Matthew's Churchgoers parade to their field day via Coal Clough Lane, August 1908

124 *Below right* Ashton-under-Lyne. The Whit Walks procession at the junction of Whitacre Road and Queen's Road then in Hurst U.D.C. U.N.C. School house in corner

125 Samuel Bamford, 1788–1872, weaver and radical reformer: son of a hand-loom weaver of Middleton, who became master of Manchester Workhouse. Bamford was arrested at Peterloo and was sent to gaol for a year. He wrote poetry and in 1844 published *Walks in South Lancashire*

126 *Right* Richard Cobden, 1804–1865:
calico printer in Manchester, who campaigned
successfully for the incorporation of Manchester
as a borough in 1838 and was a member of its
first borough council. Persuaded John Bright
to join him in the Anti-Corn Law League.
When the Corn Laws were repealed, Cobden
received a national testimonial of over £60,000.
His house in Quay Street was later used for
Owen's College

127 *Below left* Sir Joseph Whitworth, 1803–
1887, engineer and philanthropist: came to
Manchester in 1821 as a mechanic and
established his own firm in 1833. Gave his
first contribution of £3,000 a year for
engineering scholarships in 1868

128 *Below right* Donald Adamson, 1820–1890,
general manufacturing engineer, boiler maker
and iron and brass founder. Invited 76
prominent leaders to his house, The Towers,
Didsbury in June 1882 to discuss the building
of the Manchester Ship Canal, of which he
became the first chairman. He died before its
completion

129 The birth place of the first Sir Robert Peel, Bart., photographed in 1854 in Blackburn. Peel was linked with Manchester industry. He sponsored the first Factory Act of 1802 to protect pauper apprentices and that of 1819 which forbade night work for children in cotton mills

131 Winston S. Churchill at the 1907 Liberal Garden Party, Cheadle Hulme. The Liberals won the General Election of 1906 with 380 seats, as compared with 160 Conservatives, 50 Labour members and 80 Irish nationalists. They proceeded to introduce a great programme of social reform

ARTS AND CULTURE

'Go now through the length and breadth of England and Wales and where is the man, whatever his ignorance or prejudice, who will speak of the Lancashire population as depraved.' W. E. Gladstone in 1864 at the opening of the public park in Farnworth

132   Sir Charles Hallé, 1819–1895. Born in Westphalia. Invited to Manchester as 'the fittest man to stir the dormant taste for art'. Began a series of concerts in the Free Trade Hall in 1858 from which the Hallé Orchestra evolved

133 *Above* William Harrison Ainsworth, 1805–1882, novelist of Manchester. He utilised Manchester Grammar School for *Mervyn Clitheroe*, Dr Dee and Ordsall Hall for *Guy Fawkes* and Manchester Jacobites for *Manchester Rebels*

134 *Above right* Manchester Art Treasures Exhibition, 1857. 'The exhibition was opened by the Prince Consort on the 5th of May. . . . I had the Royal party right in front of me as it approached the dais prepared for Her Majesty. She looked every inch a Queen. . . . She could not help but feel the warmth of her Lancashire greeting', according to the reminiscences 1840–1905 of L. M. Hayes

135 *Below right* Opening of Bury Art Gallery, 1901

138   *Below* Waterfoot. The
Excelsior Concert Party 24 April
1910. 'The great works of Handel,
Haydn, Beethoven and Mozart
have solaced the toil of thousands
of the poorest people in
Lancashire' – Edwin Waugh
(1817–1890)

139   *Right* The Primitive
Methodist Church, King Street,
Stretford. Choir picnic, *c.* 1909

140   *Below right* Goodshaw Brass
Band, Rawtenstall, 18 July 1903

141 Rushbearing and Morris dancers, 1886, Middleton. 'In the autumn the Morris dancers came round with their attractive rush cart, a sort of house made of rushes and raised on to a lorry. It was ingeniously made' – L. M. Hayes in 1905

SPORTS AND ENTERTAINMENT

'Now in place of 70 hours a week we had 55½ hours. It became a practice, mostly on Saturdays, to play games, especially football and cricket' – according to the diary of Moses Heap, a Rossendale cotton spinner

143   Ashton-under-Lyne Cricket Club 1st XI, 1860 to 1865. Club cricket was at first a game for gentlemen. Working men were originally only permitted to field and bowl during practice at Haslingden

144 Pavilion, Cheetham Hill Cricket Club, 1883. 'In those days underhand bowling was the rule', according to the reminiscences (1840–1905) of L. M. Hayes

145 *Below* Lancashire County Cricket Team 1905
> *They keep men in Old Trafford*
> *In snowy raiment clad,*
> *To tell men when they are run out*
> *And if the light is bad –*
>   Roger Oldham, *Manchester Alphabet* (1906)

OTTELL (W)   HALLOWS J.   KERMODE (A.)   ANSON (J.)   YLDESLEY (J.T.)

H. G. GARNETT.   L.O.S POIDEVIN.   R.H. SPOONER.   A.C. MACLAREN   W. BREARLEY.   SHARP (J.)

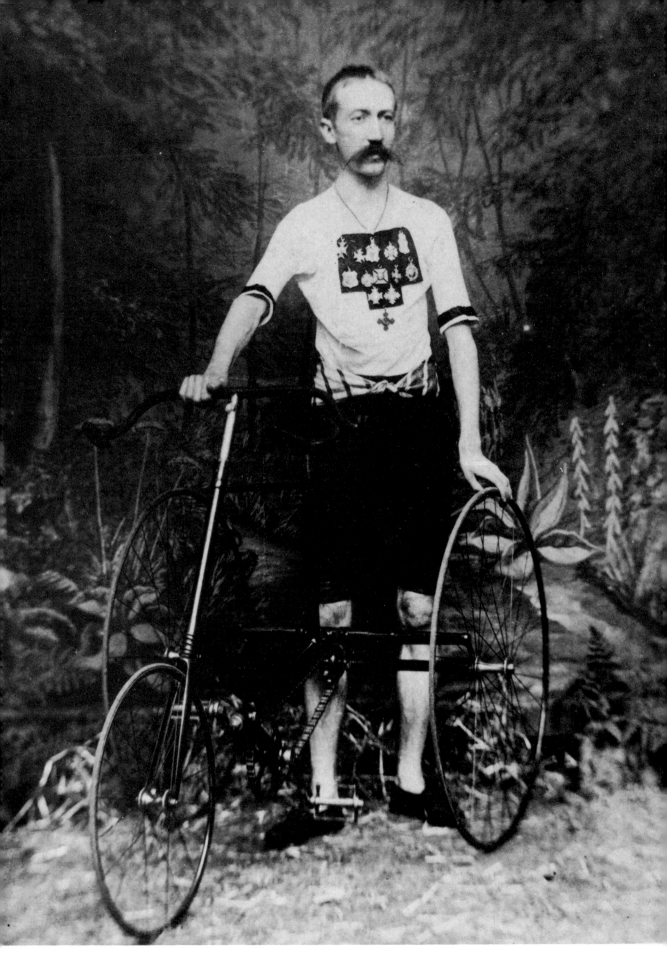

146 Rossendale Bicycle and Tricycle Club. Mr Whitworth, one of the club's founders, posing for photographs with his medals, *c.* 1890

147 Rossendale Bicycle and Tricycle Club in 1899. Founded in 1878

148 Blackburn. The boating lake in Queen's Park, 1898

149 The Playground, Henshaw's Deaf and Dumb School, Manchester

151 *Right* Belle Vue Fireworks Display. John Jennison, founder of Belle View Pleasure Gardens and Zoo, introduced a spectacular annual fireworks display in 1852

Belle View it is true
Is a very good Zoo,
Brass bands and rip raps
And set pieces too –

Roger Oldham, *Manchester Alphabet* (1906)

150 Opening of Whitaker Park, Rawtenstall, 1901

152 Manchester Racecourse (New Barns) Salford, 31 May 1901

153   Manchester Racecourse, Whitsun, 1908